بسم الله الرحمن الرحيم

IV Publishing
Email: sales@islamicvillage.co.uk
Website: www.islamicvillage.co.uk

Title: Seeking Allah through the Means of Tawassul & Istighatha
Author: Habib Kazim Al-Saqqaf
Translated by: Imran Rahim
Edited & Abridged by: Abu Zahra

ISBN: 978-0-9520853-6-2

Cover Design Concept: Dr Javed Khan

Another OUTSTANDING Production
Email: books@standoutnow.co.uk Tel: +44 (0)121 327 3277

SEEKING ALLAH

THROUGH THE MEANS OF TAWASSUL & ISTIGATHA

التَّوَسُّلُ وَالاسْتِغَاثَة

HABIB KAZIM AL-SAQQAF

TRANSLATED BY
IMRAN RAHIM

EDITED & ABRIDGED BY
ABU ZAHRA

ISLAMIC • VILLAGE

Contents

Foreword to Translation
i

Introduction
1

WHAT IS ISTIGHATHA?
4

WHAT IS TAWASSUL?
5

PART ONE
Misconceptions

MISAPPLYING QUR'ANIC VERSES
7

A DISCUSSION OF HOW THE DEAD
CAN BENEFIT THE LIVING
26

AN ERRONEOUS UNDERSTANDING OF DIVINE UNITY
30

THE MEANING OF SUPPLICATION AND WORSHIP
33

PART TWO
The Proofs of Ahl al-Sunna wa'l-Jamā'a for the Permissibility of Istighātha

THE FIRST PROOF
37

THE SECOND PROOF
39

THE THIRD PROOF
42

THE FOURTH PROOF
44

THE FIFTH PROOF
45

PART THREE
Rational Proofs for the Position of Ahl al-Sunna wa'l-Jamā'a

THE FIRST PROOF
50

THE SECOND PROOF
50

Foreword to Translation

Each and every kind of praise is for Allah. May peace and blessings be upon the immense mercy of Allah, the mercy to all creations, our liegelord Muhammad, the son of ʿAbdullah, and likewise upon his Companions, the protectors of the religion, and upon those who follow him with excellence until the Day of Recompense.

In these times especially, the Muslim community is in dire need of uniting upon the shared principles of Islam and then we must adopt a mutual love and co-operation for the sake of Allah and His Messenger ﷺ. This mutual love will not occur until clear, faith-based principles are established, amongst them having a good opinion of one another.

Perhaps the translation of this book *Seeking Allah through the Means of Tawassul & Istighātha* will be an opportunity for a Muslim to excuse his fellow Muslim if they disagree on an aspect of the religion, and perhaps it will open a door of mutual co-operation amongst the various groups, based on universally-accepted matters of the religion. We ask Allah for acceptance; benefit and guidance for mankind and honour for the Muslims.

[Ḥabīb] Mūsā Kaẓim b. Jaʿfar al-Saqqāf
10th Safar 1436 AH / 2nd December 2014 CE
Tarim, Yemen

﴿يَا أَيُّهَا الَّذِينَ آمَنُواْ اتَّقُواْ اللّهَ وَابْتَغُواْ إِلَيْهِ
الْوَسِيلَةَ وَجَاهِدُواْ فِي سَبِيلِهِ لَعَلَّكُمْ تُفْلِحُونَ﴾

O you who believe, fear Allah and seek a means to approach Him, and strive in His way in order that you may succeed

(Qur'ān 5:35)

Introduction

All praise is for Allah, the only one worthy of worship. May peace and blessings be upon our master Muhammad, the son of ʿAbdullah, the absolute slave of Allah, and upon his family and Companions and those who follow and love him.

Allah says about Himself, *He revealed to His slave that which He revealed.*[1] In this verse the exact nature of what was revealed is not mentioned to indicate how great it is.[2] So sublime is He Who gave our Prophet ﷺ such gifts that He did not give to anyone else.

I heard one of the people of knowledge, may Allah allow us to completely benefit from him, say,

---

1 Qur'ān 53:4

2 Tafsīr al-Jalālayn

"The amount that the Prophet ﷺ is elevated spiritually in every instant cannot be encompassed by the intellects of all people put together, since the reward for every act of obedience performed by every Muslim is recorded in the scrolls of his good deeds and then multiplied. He said ﷺ, 'Whoever directs someone to perform a good deed will have the same reward as the one who performs the deed.'[3]

Praise be to the Lord Who blessed us with Muhammad
and brought us out of darkness and gloom
Into the light of Islam, knowledge and wisdom,
blessings and faith, and the best of commands!

'*The best of commands*' is divine oneness which he taught us when he said, for example, 'The most truthful word spoken by a poet is the saying of Labīd: "Indeed everything save Allah is false."'[4] I heard another of the people of knowledge say – may Allah allow us to completely benefit from him – commenting on this hadith,

> Allah is the Originator Who brought everything into existence. The Master of all existent beings addressed the intelligent and attempted to alert the heedless so that they may realise the higher objective and thereby witness the Creator instead of the creation. He said in His noble address – which is a cause for people to be ennobled – as it is narrated in the *ṣaḥīḥ* collections, that the most

3 Muslim
4 Al-Bukhārī and Muslim

> truthful word spoken by a poet is that of Labīd. O Beloved of Allah, allow us to hear the words of Labīd, for it is sweeter to hear them from you. The words of Labīd were accorded the highest honour when our master Muhammad uttered them. The Leader of those who witness divine unity (*tawḥīd*) said, 'Indeed everything save Allah is false.'

This belief in divine oneness, which the Prophet ﷺ planted in the hearts of the Muslims in general, and in the people of the Arabian peninsula specifically is protected from anything that may detract from it. The evidence for this is in the statement of the Prophet ﷺ, 'Indeed the Devil has despaired of being worshipped by those in the Arabian peninsula who pray regularly, but his hope is to sow discord amongst them.'[5]

He also said ﷺ, 'Shaddād, they will not worship the sun, or a stone or an idol, but rather they will seek for their deeds to be seen by people,'[6] and, 'What I fear most for my nation is associating partners with Allah. I do not say they will worship the sun, the moon or idols, but rather actions which are performed for other than Allah, and hidden desires.'[7]

On the basis of these, and also other hadiths, it is inconceivable that the people of the Arabian peninsula who pray regularly could commit *shirk*, meaning associating partners with Allah. It is conceivable that disbelief (*kufr*) and apos-

---

5 Muslim, Aḥmad, al-Tirmidhī and ibn Mājah

6 Al-Ḥākim. There is some weakness in the hadith

7 Ibn Mājah. There is some weakness in the hadith

tasy (*riddah*) could occur, but not *shirk*, due to the explicit textual evidence. Although the hadith specifically mentions the people of the Arabian peninsula, it also applies to other Muslims whose practice and belief are the same as theirs; so it is also inconceivable that they too would commit *shirk*. Despite this, some Muslims are of the opinion that making *istighātha* and, to a lesser extent, *tawassul* constitute *shirk*.

This treatise explains the concept of *istighātha,* examines its proofs in detail and resolves areas of confusion.

- The first section deals with misconceptions relating to the concept of istighātha
- The second section mentions the [textual] proofs of Ahl al-Sunna wa'l-Jamā'a for istighātha
- The third section mentions some rational proofs for the position of Ahl al-Sunna wa'l-Jamā'a

WHAT IS ISTIGHATHA?

Istighātha linguistically means seeking assistance. Technically it is to call upon someone to assist you in order to save you from difficulty or to fulfil a need. It is well known that only Allah has the ability to give assistance. However, this does not negate the fact that Allah makes some of His slaves a means of assistance to others. Whether someone seeks assistance from Allah directly or from one of His slaves, he is in reality seeking assistance from Allah.

Linguistically, *tawassul* is to draw near to something else. One says, for example, 'so-and-so drew near (*tawassala*) to so-and-so by means of such-and-such a thing.' A *wasīla* is the means by which one draws near to something, which is the meaning of Allah's saying, '*O you who believe, fear Allah and seek a means (wasīla) to approach Him.*'[8] Technically, it is supplicating Allah by means of an intermediary, whether it be a living person, a dead person, a good deed or a name or attribute of Allah.

We ask Allah that He blesses us, our loved ones and our teachers as He blessed the sincere callers to Allah and the complete inheritors of the Prophet ﷺ, with the best of both abodes accompanied with goodness and well-being. We ask Him to benefit us by that which He has taught us and that He allows us to act upon it and that He teaches us directly, without medium. He is indeed the Most Generous and the Most Merciful.

---

8 Qur'ān 5:35

1

Misconceptions

MISAPPLYING QUR'ANIC VERSES

A REPREHENSIBLE INNOVATION THAT HAS become widespread is taking verses which were revealed regarding the idolaters and disbelievers of Mecca and applying them to the majority of Muslims. This is a trait of the Khawārij, as ibn 'Umar said. Imam al-Bukhārī mentions in his *Ṣaḥīḥ* that Ibn 'Umar considered them [the Khawārij] to be the worst of Allah's creation and would say, 'They have taken verses revealed concerning the idolaters and disbelievers and have applied them to believers.'

One of their arguments is that, as the Qur'ān says, the idolaters believe in Allah and believe that it was He who created the heavens and the earth, but despite this, they worship idols and deify them. They say that Muslims who believe in *tawassul* and *istighātha* are no different to these idolaters. The truth is, however, that there are three key differences between these idolaters and Muslims who believe in *tawassul* and *istighātha:*

1. The idolaters' belief in God will not benefit them due to their rejection of the resurrection and the other tenets of belief, such as the Pool (*ḥawḍ*), Paradise, Hellfire, the Bridge and the Last Day and the Resurrection. They can be compared to the Devil or the Jews and the Christians, all of whom believe in Allah but whose faith will not benefit them at all.

2. Alongside their belief in Allah, the disbelievers deified idols and took them as gods, as Allah says, '*Did they make their gods one God?*'[9] The Muslims who believe in *tawassul* and *istighātha,* on the other hand, do not deify anyone or anything.

3. The idolaters believed that the idols could benefit them and harm them independently of Allah. The Muslims who believe in *tawassul* and *istighātha*, however, do not believe that the righteous have the ability to benefit or harm them independently of Allah. They merely believe that the righteous are closer to Allah and thus use them as intermediaries. The difference between them and the idolaters is like the difference between the heavens and the earth.

---

9 Qur'ān 38:5

The scholars ﷺ say that it is incorrect and impermissible to use verses such as these to prohibit *istighātha* and to declare the majority of Muslims idolaters. Less than fifty verses are used as evidence for this from a total of more than one hundred and ninety verses which were revealed regarding the disbelievers and idolaters. Thus the vast majority of verses clearly show that there is no similarity between idolaters and Muslims who practise *istighātha.*

The following verses are examples of this:

> *And if you wonder, then wondrous is their saying: "What! When we become dust, shall we then be created anew?" Those are they who disbelieve in their Lord; on their necks are fetters; those shall be the people of the Fire, dwelling therein forever.*[10]

> *And they say: "What! When we become bones and dust, shall we really be raised up again and created anew?"*[11]

> *And those who disbelieve say, "We neither believe in this Qur'ān nor in that which was before it."*[12]

> *And they assign daughters to Allah. Transcendent is He! And to themselves [the sons] they desire. When one of them receives tidings [of the birth] of*

10 Qur'ān 13:5
11 Qur'ān 17:49
12 Qur'ān 34:31

a female his face darkens and he surpresses his grief. He conceals himself from people because of the bad news he has received, [asking himself]: "Shall he keep her and be ashamed, or bury her beneath the soil" Evil indeed is their judgment! [13]

Such people use the following verses as evidence that the disbelievers of Quraysh were in fact monotheists who believed in Allah's oneness as the Creator and the Sustainer, the Giver of Life and Death.

And if you were to ask them: "Who created the heavens and the earth, and subjected the sun and the moon?" They would say: "Allah." Why then are they lying? [14]

Say: "Who is it that provides for you from the sky and the earth, or who possesses hearing and sight; and who brings forth the living from the dead and the dead from the living, and who directs all affairs?" They will say: "Allah!" So say: "Will you not then fear [Him]?" [15]

If you ask them: "Who has created the heavens and the earth?" they will answer: "The August, the Knowing has created them." [16]

---

13 Qur'ān 16:57-59
14 Qur'ān 29:61
15 Qur'ān 10: 31
16 Qur'ān 43: 9

The answer to their claim is this: these verses do not confirm the faith of the disbelievers such that it can be used as a proof for their belief in Allah's lordship (*rubūbiyya*). Rather they only made such statements whenever the Prophet ﷺ presented proofs for the existence of Allah and His right to be worshipped and they were unable to respond.

Sayyid Ḥasan al-Saqqāf says in his book, *al-Tanḍīḍ*,

> When the Prophet ﷺ would prove to them Allah's existence and oneness, and that there is no god besides Him, and thus tell them that they should stop worshipping and prostrating to idols, they would feel cornered and were unable to provide a response. When asked by the Prophet ﷺ, "Who created the heavens and the earth?" they would reply, "Allah." And they would argue that their worshipping idols was merely to draw them closer to Allah. Their claim however was false, as Allah immediately contested by saying, '*Allah does not guide the lying rejecter.*'[17]
>
> Allah never legislated idol worship for these disbelievers in order for them to draw close to Him, so how could they draw close to Allah through something that has not been legislated? Rather, they were prohibited from doing so, and Allah ﷻ sent His Prophet ﷺ to nullify this. Therefore their claim that they did so to draw closer to Allah is entirely false.

---

17 Qur'ān 39: 3

What further serves to negate this claim is that the disbelievers made it clear that they worshipped idols – which they believed to be gods. However, when Muslims use the Prophet ﷺ or any of the prophets or saints as intermediaries they do not worship them. They do not believe them to gods but rather slaves ennobled by Allah. Thus statements made by idolaters regarding their idols in the Qur'ān such as '*We worship them only that they may bring us closer to Allah*'[18] cannot be applied to Muslims who make *tawassul* and *istighātha*.

The 'faith' of the disbelievers was merely superficial and cannot be considered real without submission to Allah and obedience to His commands. This is confirmed by the verse,

> *And if you ask them who created the heavens*
> *and the earth, they will say: "Allah."*
> *Say: "Do you not think then, of those you*
> *worship beside Allah, if Allah willed some harm*
> *for me, could they remove from me His harm;*
> *or if He willed some mercy for me, could they*
> *restrain His mercy?"*[19]

Imam Ibn Kathīr ﷺ said,

> This means that the idolaters would admit that Allah ﷻ is the Creator of all things but despite this, they would worship others besides Him, who had no power to benefit them or harm them. For this reason, Allah said, '*Do you not think then,*

18 Qur'ān 39:3
19 Qur'ān 39:38

> *of those you worship beside Allah, if Allah willed some harm for me, could they remove from me His harm…*' meaning, after you have confirmed that the creator of the celestial and earthly realms is Allah, then tell me about your gods. If Allah had willed that some harm befall me, are they able to ward off this harm, or tribulation and repel it?

Allah thus refutes their claims to faith in all of these verses, due to their worshipping idols.

Therefore the superficial 'faith' of the disbelievers cannot be called faith and cannot be compared to the true faith of those who make *tawassul* and *istighātha*. Imam Fakhr al-Dīn al-Rāzī mentions an opinion that all people have an intrinsic knowledge of the existence of an all-powerful and wise God and the natural disposition of the intellect bears witness to the soundness of this knowledge.[20]

Sheikh al-Ṣābūnī says in his summary of Ibn Kathīr's exegesis regarding the verse, '*And if you ask them who created the heavens and earth, and who subjugated the sun and the moon, they will say: "Allah." How are they then deluded (such that they do not follow the truth)?*'[21]

> The meaning is that Allah ﷻ created them as a clear indication that the ability to create is specific to Allah, which points to the fact that primordial faith is embedded within the natural disposi-

20 al-Rāzī, *al-Tafsīr al-Kabīr*, commenting on verse 29:61

21 Qur'ān 29:61

> tion of man, as the verse states, '*The primordial nature of Allah upon which man was created.*'[22] The Prophet ﷺ said, "Every child is born upon the natural disposition."[23]

Do such people therefore believe that the various types of disbelievers such as those who worship cows, and fire and trees (and even atheists) are like the disbelievers of Quraysh and believe in Allah's oneness as a Lord (*tawḥīd rubūbiyya*)? The vast majority of people know of the existence of the Omnipotent, Wise God, as mentioned earlier by Imam Fakhr al-Rāzī ؓ. Yet are they thereby superior to Muslims who practice *tawassul*? Can a rational Muslim really say such a thing?

It should be clear then that this type of faith was not unique to the disbelievers of Quraysh. Rather it is something that all types of disbelievers innately possess. The word 'faith' can only be applied here in its linguistic sense and it cannot be said that those disbelievers truly believe in Allah.

This has been approved by Imam al-Nawawī, whose rank and knowledge is undisputed, may Allah benefit us by him and likewise all of the scholars and inheritors. He says in his commentary on *Ṣaḥīḥ Muslim*[24] that someone can only be truly called a believer when he believes in his heart,

---

22 Qur'ān 30:30

23 Narrated by al-Bukhārī and others. The remainder of the hadith is, 'And his parents make him a Jew, or a Christian or a Magian.'

24 p.147, vol. 1

affirms that belief with his tongue and then acts according to the dictates of that belief with his limbs.

He goes on to say:

> Everyone is in agreement that if a person were to declare his faith with his tongue and then to act without knowledge of his Lord, he would not be entitled to be called a believer. If he were to know Him, and acted upon this but rejected with his tongue and denied what he knew of divine oneness, he would not warrant being called a believer. Likewise, if he affirmed belief in Allah ﷻ and His Messengers but did not perform the obligatory acts of Islam he would not called a believer.[25] In the Arabic language he would be called a believer due to his affirmation, but he would nevertheless not warrant the term 'believer' in Allah's sight, due to His saying, '*Verily the believers are those whom, when Allah is mentioned, their hearts quiver and when His verses are recited, they are increased in faith, and upon their Lord do they rely. They are those who establish the prayer and give out from that with which We have given them.*' [26] Our Lord ﷻ has thus informed us that the believer is someone who possesses these qualities.

---

25 This is if the person rejects the obligatory nature of the act, not if he merely leaves the act itself– Tr.

26 Qur'ān 8:2-3

If we were to look at the three types of people mentioned by Imam al-Nawawī, we would find that even those who have the worst outcome of the three are better than the disbelievers of Quraysh. But despite this, they still do not warrant the term 'believers.' So how then can the disbelievers of Quraysh be worthy of the term 'believers?' They may have affirmed their belief with their tongues but they disbelieved in the Prophet ﷺ and in the Last Day and rejected the names of Allah ﷻ, as in the verse, '*And they disbelieve in the Most-Compassionate.*'[27]

Sheikh al-Ṣābūnī says,

> '*And they disbelieve in the Most-Compassionate*', meaning that this nation to which We have sent you, disbelieve in the Most-Compassionate. This is because they haughtily rejected the attributes of Allah, the Most-Merciful, the Most-Compassionate. For this reason, they refused to write, 'In the name of Allah the Most-Merciful, the Most-Compassionate,' on the day of Ḥudaybiya saying, 'We do not know what the Most-Merciful, the Most-Compassionate is.'[28]

Other verses that are fallaciously used as proof to declare Muslims as idolaters include,

> *'And those to whom you supplicate instead of Him do not possess even the skin of a date-stone.*

27 Qur'ān 13:30

28 Narrated by al-Bukhārī

If you were to supplicate to them, they hear not your prayer, and if they were to hear you they would not [be able to] answer you, and on the Day of Arising they will reject your association of them [with Allah]. And none can inform you like the One Who is Aware.'[29]

Such people apply these verses and similar verses to people of pure faith who make *tawassul* and mistakenly think that Muslims worship the inhabitants of these graves when supplicating there. They say, 'These grave-dwellers who you call upon rather than Allah do not possess even the skin of a date-stone and they cannot hear your prayers and if even if they could, they would not be able to answer you because they are unable to benefit you and because the dead cannot benefit the living. On the Day of Resurrection, they will disown your association of them with Allah.'

The answer to such accusations is that these verses were revealed in reference to people worshipping idols and not people in their graves. Imam al-Suyūṭī says in his commentary on the Qur'ān that '*those unto whom you pray instead of Him*' means 'you worship other than Him, meaning idols.'[30]

A similar explanation is given by Sheikh al-Ṣābūnī in *Ṣafwat al-Tafāsīr*,

> Therefore it is not permissible to apply these verses, which were revealed in relation to idols,

29 Qur'ān 35:13-14

30 Qur'ān 35:13

to people in their graves. The people of the grave are the antithesis of those about whom the verses were revealed, as they have their righteous deeds which they earned in the world and by which they benefit.

As for the idols, they own nothing as they are inanimate objects and they do not hear anyone who calls out to them, whereas the deceased hear those who call out to them. This is narrated in *ṣaḥīḥ* hadiths which are clear in meaning, such as the hadith narrated by al-Bukhārī and Muslim, "Indeed the deceased one, when he is placed in his grave, hears the footsteps (of the people burying him)." Another example is the hadith in Bukhārī and Muslim which narrates how the Prophet ﷺ called out to 'the People of the Pit'[31] and 'Umar b. al-Khaṭṭāb questioned his action. The Prophet ﷺ then said, "By the One in whose hand is the soul of Muhammad, you do not hear what I am saying to them better than they do."[32]

Another example is the *ṣaḥīḥ* hadith narrated by al-Ṭabarānī in which the Prophet ﷺ was asked if the

---

31 The dead disbelievers of Quraysh who were buried in a pit after the Battle of Badr

32 In other words, 'they can hear what I am saying just as well as you can.'

deceased hear. He replied, 'They hear just as you hear, but they do not reply.'[33]

A further example is the *ṣaḥīḥ* hadith in which the Prophet ﷺ said, 'None of you passes by the grave of his brother in faith who he knew in this life, and greets him with peace except that he recognises him and returns the greeting.'[34] These are just some of the hadiths which affirm that the deceased hear, which dispel any doubt.

Verses such as, '*But you can never make those who are in the graves hear*'[35] and, *You cannot make the dead, nor the deaf hear your call*'[36] are used as proof that the dead cannot hear. However, what is negated in such verses is not the ability of the dead to hear but rather the ability to take heed and thus be guided. Many verses of the Qur'ān reinforce this meaning – that although the disbelievers can hear, see and speak, their hearing, sight and speech are not means for them to be guided. Examples of this are the verse, '*You will see them gazing at you but they do not see,*'[37] and also, '*deaf, dumb and blind, they do not understand.*'[38]

Imam al-Suyūṭī said in his didactic poem on faith,

The fact that the dead hear the speech of people is

---

33 Hadith no. 6715 in *Mu'jam al-Kabār* of al-Ṭabarānī – Tr.

34 Ibn 'Abd al-Barr narrates this from Ibn 'Abbās and graded it as *ṣaḥīḥ*, along with others. – Tr.

35 Qur'ān 27:80

36 Qur'ān 35:22

37 Qur'ān 7:197

38 Qur'ān 2:171

> *Unequivocally transmitted to us through reports in books,*
>
> *And the meaning of verses which [appear to] negate this is heeding the call of guidance:*
> *They neither accept not listen to that which benefits them*

Therefore it is utterly false and incorrect to use verses which were revealed regarding disbelievers to accuse Muslims of idolatry.

Someone might say: what about the principle in legal theory which states that the universality of the statement is given precedence over the specific circumstance in which it was revealed or the context in which it was mentioned?

The answer lies in the words of Shaykh Abdullah al-Ghumārī in *al-Radd al-Muḥkam al-Matīn*:

> Verses which were revealed regarding the Arab idolaters are not specific to them merely because they were revealed due to them. In fact they apply to every person who worships something besides Allah, and takes it as a god along with Allah, regardless of whether he is an Arab or a non-Arab, and regardless of whether this takes place during the period of revelation or thereafter until the Final Hour. This is because the word 'idolaters' in the verse encompasses such a person both in its legal and linguistic usage. The fact that it was revealed regarding a specific group of them, that

is the idolaters from the Arabs, does not prevent it from applying to others, nor is there a contradiction.

One must therefore take the linguistic signification and hold to its general application until there is evidence that suggests it should applied specifically. An example of this is the word 'water' in the hadith of Tirmidhī in which the Prophet ﷺ was asked about water from the Well of Bida'a, and he ﷺ said, 'Nothing causes pure water to become impure.' This does not only apply to the well of Bida'a because it is mentioned here, but rather it includes all water from wells and rivers because the word 'water' includes all of these linguistically and legally.

Similarly, the word 'Muslim' in the saying of the Prophet ﷺ, 'A Muslim does not become impure.' This does not refer to Abū Hurayra ؓ alone, who was the subject of this narration, but rather it includes every Muslim from that time until the Final Hour.

Likewise, every general word which is mentioned due to a specific reason is to be understood generally, meaning that the word is applied to anything that conforms to its meaning linguistically and legally.

It cannot, however, be applied to that which does not conform to its meaning, such as interpreting the word 'Muslim' in the previous hadith to include both a Muslim and a disbeliever. This is a complete misapplication of the word since its use does not conform to its linguistic and legal meaning. Furthermore, this is a form of manipulation of the legal sources.

If someone were to say, 'I did not intend by the actions of the idolaters merely association and taking gods beside Allah, rather I intended both that and that which it implies, such as calling out to the pious, seeking their assistance (*istighātha)* and using them as intermediaries (*tawassul*) in order to fulfil needs, since all of this is in accordance with the meaning of association. Therefore the verses apply to those that make *tawassul* by the general meaning of the word, and nothing else.'

We would say this is erroneous from various perspectives:

Firstly, the reality of association (*ishrāk*) linguistically is something entirely different from *tawassul*, *istighātha* and supplication because the meaning of *ishrāk* is the belief that Allah has a partner in His godhood which constitutes disbelief. For this reason, many linguists have explained *ishrāk* as disbelief as it constitutes disbelief in Allah and denial of His oneness.

As for *tawassul*, it is drawing near to something else. One says for example, 'so-and-so drew near (*tawassala*) to so-and-so by means of such-and-such a thing.' The *wasīla* is the means by which one draws near to something, as in Allah saying, '*O you who believe, fear Allah and seek a means (wasīla) to approach Him.*' [39]

Istighātha is seeking help (*ghawth*) and assistance (*najda*). Allah says, '*The one who was from his group sought help (istighātha) from him against the one who was from his enemies.*' [40]

*Du*ᶜ*ā* (supplication) means to call out and to seek someone's attention; it is said, 'He called out (*da*ᶜ*ā*) to so-and-so, meaning he called out to him seeking his attention. (Allah says), '*Do not make your address [du*ᶜ*ā'] to the Messenger like your address to one another.*' [41] And one says, 'He called out to Allah," meaning he called out to Him with sincerity and humility. '*And when my slaves ask about Me, then I am indeed near. I answer the supplication (du*ᶜ*ā) of the one who supplicates when he supplicates.*' [42]

As you can see, all of these realities are different, so how could it be correct to intend one meaning alone? Can this be anything other than manipulation of the sacred texts?

Secondly, the association in which the idolaters took part, for which the Qur'ān rebukes them, was

39 Qur'ān 5:35
40 Qur'ān 28.15
41 Qur'ān 24.63
42 Qur'ān 2.186

> their worship of prophets, angels and saints based upon their belief that they shared in Allah's godhood (*ulūhiyya*), and that they were able to have a direct effect upon things. For this reason, when the Qur'ān rebukes them it mentions the evidence for Allah's oneness. There are many verses of the Qur'ān which talk about Allah's oneness (*tawḥīd*) and refute the idolaters but you will not find in them a single reference to *tawassul* according to the meaning that is being discussed here because it was not a practice of the idolaters. Therefore it is incorrect to say that such verses could apply to *tawassul*, be it generally (*'umūm*), specifically (*khuṣūṣ*) or by any type of denotation (*dilālāt*).
>
> Thirdly, the practice of *istighātha* has been narrated in hadith as will be mentioned and this is conclusive proof that it is not *shirk*.

It should now be clear that the verses which are used as evidence to prohibit *istighātha* are used erroneously as they have no relevance to this discussion. You will not find a single reliable Qur'ānic commentator (*mufassir*) using these verses as proofs for the prohibition of *tawassul* or *istighātha*.

Some people use the hadith of Sayyiduna Abū Bakr narrated by al-Ṭabarānī in *al-Mu'jam al-Kabīr* as evidence to prohibit *istighātha*. In the hadith, Sayyiduna Abū Bakr said, 'Let us seek help (*nastaghīth*) from the Messenger of Allah ﷺ.' The Messenger of Allah said, 'Help is not sought through me. Help is only to be sought from Allah (the

Exalted).' Using this as proof to prohibit *istighātha* is false because the hadith's chain of narration contains Ibn Lihī'a and his reliability as a narrator is subject to doubt (*mutakallam fīhi*) amongst the scholars of hadith.

For such a serious matter as declaring Muslims idolaters, one cannot rely upon a weak narration. Besides this, no rational person would consider Abū Bakr al-Ṣiddīq ؓ ignorant of the difference between *shirk* and *tawḥīd* since he was amongst the first to accept Islam and believe in the Messenger ﷺ and he then spent many years in his company. Had *istighātha* of the Messenger of Allah ﷺ been *shirk*, then why would Abū Bakr al-Ṣiddīq have done this, when he was one of the most knowledgeable of the Companions?

If the hadith were authentic, then the only way to interpret the Prophet's statement, 'Help is not sought through me' is to understand it literally [43] in the same way that we understand the verse, *And you did not throw when you threw, but it was Allah who threw.*[44]

Furthermore, if the hadith were authentic it would destroy the erroneous claim that *istighātha* is permissible if one seeks the help of a living person but impermissible if one calls upon the dead. We find that when people are unable to reject the evidence in favour of *istighātha*, they say, '*Istighātha* is permissible through the living according to their ability, but not the dead.' There is no doubt in

---

43   Meaning that even if you seek assistance from a human being, you are in reality seeking assistance from Allah
44   Qur'ān 8:17

the context of this hadith that the Messenger of Allah ﷺ was able to supplicate and was able to take other measures to help people. It is thus illogical to say that *istighātha* is permissible with the living and then say it is completely forbidden on the basis of this hadith.

A DISCUSSION OF HOW THE DEAD CAN BENEFIT THE LIVING

Some people claim that the dead cannot benefit the living but this claim is false. The belief of *Ahl al-Sunna wa'l-Jamā'a* is that nothing can cause benefit or harm except Allah, and that neither a living person nor a dead person can benefit anyone independently of Allah. If Allah wishes to benefit you through a living person, this person benefits you figuratively by his speech and his actions. The One who is truly benefiting you is Allah ﷻ.

If Allah wishes to benefit you by a dead person, this person benefits you figuratively by supplicating for you or by something else, according to his rank with Allah ﷻ. Allah says about His chosen slaves in the hadith *qudsī*, "And if he asks of Me, I will surely give him [what he asks]."

This includes a supplication for himself or for someone else, whether this is in the worldly life (*dunyā*) or in the intermediary realm (*barzakh*) as the actual bringer of benefit is Allah. For this reason, Allah ﷻ said to the Prophet ﷺ, '*And you did not throw when you threw, rather it was Allah who threw.*'[45] It is known that it was the Beloved Muhammad ﷺ

45 Qur'ān 8:17

who threw, and Allah affirmed him as the one who figuratively threw but He ascribed the actual throwing to Himself. He ﷻ said, '*Allah created you and that which you do.*'[46]

For this reason, the belief of *Ahl al-Sunna wa'l-Jamā'a* is that water itself does not quench a person's thirst, a knife does not cut by itself, a fire does not burn by itself and medicine does not cure by itself. It is only Allah ﷻ who causes people's thirst to be quenched when they drink water, and causes cutting to take place when a knife makes contact with something, and causes burning to take place when fire touches something and causes a cure to take place when medicine is taken. Things generally occur due to cause and effect, but this is not always the case – it is possible for something to come about without a cause or for the cause not to bring about the normal effect.

Evidence to support the fact that the dead can benefit the living if Allah wills can be found in the hadith narrated by al-Bukhārī in his *Ṣaḥīḥ* collection regarding the Ascension. After Allah made fifty prayers obligatory upon our Prophet Muhammad ﷺ, he met the Prophet Mūsā ﷺ in the sixth heaven. Mūsā told the Prophet Muhammad ﷺ to return to his Lord in order that the number of prayers be reduced. So the Prophet ﷺ Muhammad went back to his Lord and continued to do so until the number was reduced from fifty to five. Thus Mūsā ﷺ benefited the nation of the Prophet Muhammad despite the fact that he was in the *barzakh* and was no longer alive on the earth.

---

46 Qur'ān 37:96

Tirmidhī narrates a similar narration in which the Prophet Ibrāhīm ﷺ informed the Prophet Muhammad ﷺ on the night of the Ascension, 'O Muhammad, convey my greetings of peace to your nation, and inform them that the soil of Paradise is pure, its water is sweet, it has flat plains which are free of vegetation[47] and its seeds are *subḥānAllāh*, *al-ḥamdulillāh*, *lā ilāha illAllāh*, *Allāhu akbar*.'

Many a Muslim has heard this hadith for the first time and tried to act upon it, or heard it for a second or third time and it aroused in him a desire for worship and remembrance and warded off laziness. All of this is by virtue of Ibrāhīm ﷺ after his departure from this worldly abode.

It is therefore clear that should Allah wish to benefit someone via a dead person, He may do so. This is because the One Who brings benefit in reality is Allah, and the dead person is only a means through which Allah causes benefit to take place.

Further evidence of the fact that the deceased are aware of the affairs of the living and may benefit them is provided by Ḥabīb Muhammad b. Sālim b. Ḥafīẓ[48] in his book, *al-Wasīla*. In it he says,

> We shall narrate a story the soundness of which is not in question. It is narrated by al-Bukhārī[49]

47 Mubārakpūrī explains the word *qi'ān* as this in his commentary on *Jāmi' al-Tirmidhī* entitled *Tuḥfat al-Aḥwadhī* – Tr.

48 The martyred father of Ḥabīb 'Umar b. Ḥafīẓ – Tr.

49 Bukhārī has mentioned this in the Book of Warfare and Expeditions (Chapter of Burial Preparation after Death)

in a summarized from, and by al-Ṭabarānī in full on the authority of Anas ؓ who said, 'When the Muslims retreated on the Day of Yamāma, I said to Thābit b. Qays, "Uncle, do you not see [what is happening]?" I found him applying a perfume normally used for the deceased (i.e. he was preparing for martyrdom in battle) and he said, "…This is not how we used to fight with the Messenger of Allah ﷺ. You have made your contemporaries accustomed to something blameworthy. O Allah, I absolve myself from the beliefs of those people [the disbelievers] and I absolve myself from the actions of those people [the Muslims]." Then he fought on until he was killed. He was wearing a valuable coat of armour and a Muslim man passed by and took it.

Some time later, when one of the Muslims was sleeping Thābit appeared to him in his dream and said, "I come to you with a bequest. Beware of saying this is a mere dream and ignoring it. When I was killed so-and-so took my armour and his tent is at the edge of the camp and there is a certain type of horse next to his tent. An inverted pot has been placed over the armour and there is a saddle on top of the pot. Go to Khālid [bin Walīd, the Muslim leader] and tell him to come and take it and tell him to say to Abū Bakr that I have a debt amounting to such and such, and that so-and-so

> [one of his slaves] is now free. The man woke up and went to Khālid and told him. Khālid sent someone to bring the armour. He told Abū Bakr of his dream and Abū Bakr executed his bequest.
>
> This deceased man was angry at the fact that his property had been taken by someone other than his rightful inheritor, so he ordered someone to go to the leader of the army to tell him of the item's exact location, so that it be returned to its rightful inheritor. He also told him to inform the Caliph, so that he could pay back his debt, and to likewise inform him that he made a bequest to free his slave. He described the place where the armour was hidden, as if he had actually witnessed the place. So reflect on this.' [50]

Based on this, you can see that the deceased may benefit the living if Allah so wishes, and death does not prevent them from this.

AN ERRONEOUS UNDERSTANDING OF DIVINE UNITY

Some Muslims have an erroneous understanding of divine unity. They claim that divine unity should be classified into

50 The author has re-worded the quotation

three parts: unity in lordship (*tawḥīd al-rubūbiyya*), unity in godhood (*tawḥīd al-ulūhiyya*), and unity in names and attributes (*asmā wa ṣifāt*). This classification is impermissible and there is no legal evidence for it.

In *al-Tanḍīḍ bi man ʿaddada'l-Tawḥīd* , Sayyid Ḥasan al-Saqqāf rejects the evidence brought to prove classification of belief into three parts. In it he says, 'The divine oneness which the Messenger ﷺ taught is pure unity and this classification [into three parts] is an invented and reprehensible innovation in religion.'

Ḥabīb Muhammad b. Sālim b. Ḥafīẓ said in *al-Wasīlah* refuting those who divide *tawḥīd*,

> Essentially, the Qur'ān is replete with instances in which the Lord (*al-Rabb*) is called God (*ilāh*) and God is called the Lord, for they allude to the same meaning. The idolater inevitably associates partners with Allah in His lordship and worships false gods. The evidence for this is that the statement, 'there is no deity save Allah' affirms unity in lordship and godhood. If it were only unity in godhood, as they say, it would necessitate that

there be another statement for lordship,[51] and no-one would suggest this.

Sayyid Aḥmad Zaynī al-Daḥlān ؓ says the following in his book, *al-Durar al-Saniyyah*,

> As for their saying that divine unity is of two types – unity in lordship (*tawḥīd rubūbiyya*) and unity in godhood (*tawḥīd ulūhiyya*) – this is likewise false because unity in lordship (*tawḥīd rubūbiyya*) is the same as unity in godhood (*tawḥīd ulūhiyya*). Do you not see how Allah said, *Am I not your Lord?*[52] He did not say, "Am I not your God?" He was content for them to affirm the oneness of His lordship. It is obvious that whoever affirms Allah's lordship affirms Allah's godhood by default since there is no lord other than God. They are one and the same thing.
>
> In the hadith, it is mentioned that the two angels question the slave in his grave, saying, "Who is your lord (*rabb*)?" They do not say, "Who is your god (*ilāh*)?" This proves that unity in lordship (*tawḥīd rubūbiyya*) is the same as unity in godhood (*tawḥīd ulūhiyya*).

---

51 Meaning it would necessary for there to be additional declaration of faith, namely *Lā Rabb illAllāh* – Tr.
52 Qurʾān 7:172

He later goes on to say,

> Have the Muslims heard the hadiths and accounts of the Bedouin Arabs who came to the Prophet ﷺ to accept Islam at his hands? Did he explain unity in lordship (*tawḥīd rubūbiyya*) and unity in godhood (*tawḥīd ulūhiyya*) and inform them that only unity in godhood (*tawḥīd ulūhiyya*) would make them enter the fold of Islam? Or rather, did he accept their outward declaration of the two testimonies of faith, and thereby consider them Muslims? What a slanderous, false testimony against Allah and His Messenger ﷺ!
>
> Whoever declares the oneness of the Lord (*rabb*), declares the oneness of God (*ilāh*) and whoever associates partners with the Lord, does so with God. Muslims have no lord except God. So when they say, 'there is no deity save Allah' they profess belief that He is their Lord and they deny any other godhood except His, just as they deny any other lordship except His, and they affirm the oneness of His essence, attributes and acts.

THE MEANING OF SUPPLICATION AND WORSHIP

A further claim that some people make is that calling out to the deceased is regarded as worshipping other than Allah and is therefore impermissible. They use the following verse as evidence for this: '*And the mosques belong to Allah so do not supplicate to anyone besides Allah.*'[53]

The meaning of this verse, as al-Baghawī mentions on the authority of Qatāda, is that when the Jews and the Christians would enter their synagogues and churches they would commit idolatry, so Allah ordered the believers to make their worship and supplications to Allah alone when they entered mosques. So their use of this verse as a proof to declare Muslims idolaters is incorrect.

A further piece of evidence which they use is the hadith of the Prophet ﷺ that '*Duʿā'* (calling upon Allah or supplication) is the essence of worship.'[54] They deduce from this that calling out to a dead person is an act of worship and constitutes idolatry.

The scholars say that calling out is not an act of worship unless the person calling out believes that the one he is calling out to has qualities of lordship, such as having the ability to bring about benefit or harm independently of Allah. When the Muslim supplicates his Lord, he believes his Lord is deserving of such sincere supplication. This hadith does not apply to a Muslim who calls out to a deceased person.

The permissibility of calling out to the deceased has been firmly established. Bukhārī and Muslim narrate, for example, that the Prophet ﷺ called out to the People of the

---

53 Qur'ān 72:18

54 Narrated by Aḥmad and others and it has been declared sound by al-Ḥākim and al-Dhahabī concurred

Pit by their names.[55] Bukhārī narrates that Abū Bakr called out to the Prophet ﷺ after his death saying, 'By my father and mother, O Prophet of Allah, Allah will not cause you to die twice.'[56]

If supplication were worship in every instance, or if calling out to the deceased were forbidden or idolatry as is mistakenly claimed, then the Prophet ﷺ would not have called out to someone deceased and Abū Bakr would not have called out to the Prophet ﷺ after his death. It is true to say that Abū Bakr did not ask the Prophet ﷺ for anything when he addressed him, but the Prophet ﷺ himself taught his nation to ask him after his death, the evidence for which we shall mention. The practice of the Companions was to make *istighātha* with the Prophet ﷺ after his death – so it is impossible for this to even remotely resemble idolatry, much less constitute idolatry. Above all the hadith proves that calling out to the deceased is permissible and is neither sinful nor idolatry.

---

55 The Prophet ﷺ to the idolaters who were killed in the Battle of Badr and subsequently buried in a pit, 'Have you found what your Lord promised you to be true?' So it was said to him, 'Are you calling upon the deceased?', so [the Prophet ﷺ] replied, 'You do not hear what I am saying to them better than them. They do not, however, reply.'

56 The scholars offer different interpretations for this statement. Ibn Ḥajār al-'Asqalānī says that the clearest interpretation is that Abū Bakr was refuting those who claimed that the Prophet ﷺ would be brought back to life because this would necessitate him dying a second time, and Allah would not cause His Prophet ﷺ to experience this. Another interpretation is that the Prophet, having already endured the suffering of death, will not endure any further suffering.

What conclusively proves that it is impossible for *du'ā'* to be considered worship in every instance is the verse, '*Do not make your calling [du'ā'] of the Messenger among yourselves as the call of one of you to another.*'[57] If calling out *du'ā'* were to be worship in every instance, then the meaning of the verse would be, 'Do not make your calling (*du'ā'*) of the Messenger among yourselves as the call of one of you to another.' It is obvious that the Companions did not worship the Messenger ﷺ, such that they needed to be forbidden from doing so.

Sayyiduna Nūḥ ﷺ says in the Qur'ān, My Lord, '*I have called*[58] *my people night and day.*'[59] Does this mean he worshipped his people, since supplication is the same as worship?

---

57 Qur'ān 24:63

58 The word used here is *da'awtu*, from the same root as *du'ā*.

59 Qur'ān 71:5

2

The Proofs of Ahl al-Sunna wa'l-Jamā'a for the Permissibility of Istighātha

THE FIRST PROOF

BUKHĀRĪ NARRATES THAT THE PROPHET ﷺ said, 'The sun will draw close on the Day of Rising until sweat reaches half-way up people's ears. Whilst this is happening, they will seek help (*istaghāthū*) from Ādam, then Mūsā, then Muhammad ﷺ who will seek intercession, and then judgement will be made amongst creation.'

The point of note here is that here is an explicit reference to *istighātha* by other than Allah in an affair over which only Allah has power, so if it were *shirk* then Allah would not have legislated it for us and been content with it for us when He says in the Qur'ān, '*If you disbelieve, Allah is free of need from you, but He is not content with disbelief for*

His slaves. If you show gratitude, then He is pleased with it for you.'[60]

Ibn Ḥajar says in *Fatḥ al-Bārī* that in regard to making *tawassul* by the Prophets that people will be in the same state in the next life as they are in this life. This shows that according to him, there is no difference between *tawassul* and *istighātha*, because the word used in the hadith is '*istaghāthū,*' but he uses the word '*tawassul.*' The scholars have said that there is ultimately no difference between supplicating Allah by means of an intermediary (*tawassul*), calling upon someone to assist you (*istighātha*), directing oneself to Allah through someone (*tawajjuh*) or seeking someone's intercession (*tashaffu'*) since they essentially amount to the same thing. The only difference between these terms is linguistic.

If someone were to say that the Prophet ﷺ informed us about this type of *istighātha*, and that the Prophets on that day will be alive and *istighātha* will be made by the living and *istighātha* is permissible by the living in this world and in the hereafter, then it is as if you are saying that an action which you regard to be *shirk* which removes a person from the fold of Islam in the realm of legal responsibility in this life is in fact permissible in the next life. This is akin to saying, for example, that you believe it is permissible for someone to pray two units of prayer whilst in this world but it is not permissible to pray them in the intermediary realm (*barzakh*) or in the hereafter.

---

60 Qur'ān 39.7

This is inconceivable because if *istighātha* constituted worship –which can only be performed for Allah's sake– then how can it be permissible to call upon a person when they are alive and it be considered *shirk* after they die? How can it be permissible by the Prophet ﷺ and *shirk* by the other Prophets and the saints? Allah is not content for His slaves to commit *shirk* in this life, in death, in this world, or in the hereafter, whether the object of that *shirk* be a prophet or an angel.

THE SECOND PROOF

'The Hadith of the Blind Man' establishes the permissibility of seeking assistance from the dead (making *istighātha)* as long as the person doing so does not believe that the dead person can bring benefit or harm independently of Allah.

Ibn Abī Khaythama narrates in his *Musnad* with his chain of transmission on the authority of 'Uthmān ibn Ḥunayf that he said,

> 'A blind man came to the Prophet ﷺ and said, "My eyesight has been afflicted so supplicate Allah for me." [The Prophet ﷺ] said, "Go and make ablution and perform two units of prayer and say, 'O Allah, I ask You and I direct myself to You through the Prophet Muhammad, the Prophet of Mercy. O Muhammad, I seek your intercession to my Lord to return my sight. O Allah, accept my intercession for myself, and accept the intercession

of my Prophet in returning my sight' and if you have a need, then do as you have done." Allah then returned his sight.'

In the narration of al-Tirmidhī from the Chapter of Invocations, it is mentioned,

> 'So he ordered him to perfect his ablution and to make the following supplication: O Allah, I ask You and I direct myself to You through Your Prophet Muhammad, the Prophet of Mercy. O Muhammad, through you I direct myself to my Lord regarding this need of mine so that it may be fulfilled. O Allah, accept his intercession for me!".'

This hadith is a clear indication of the permissibility of seeking assistance (*istighātha*) from the Prophet ﷺ after his passing specifically, and from other prophets and saints. This is because the Prophet ﷺ taught the man to seek his assistance by saying, 'O Muhammad.' This is calling someone who is not present and it is not specific to his lifetime, as the Prophet ﷺ knew that his people would do this after him especially since he said in the narration of Ibn Abī Khaythama – 'and if you have a need, then do as you have done.'

Had this only been permissible during the lifetime of the Prophet ﷺ, but then considered *shirk* after his passing, then the Prophet ﷺ would have warned his Companions against doing this after his passing. Had this only been permissible while in the presence of the Prophet ﷺ he would have clarified this. Had it been specific to the Prophet ﷺ, there would have been an indication that this was specific to him.

The scholars have compiled works of *khaṣā'iṣ,* which list the unique characteristics of the Messenger ﷺ, such as his being allowed to marry more than four women simultaneously and his perpetual fasting.[61] No recognised scholar, however, has mentioned in any of these books that one of the Prophet's unique characteristics is that it is permissible to seek his assistance (*istighātha*) during his life, but not after his passing, or that it is permissible to seek his assistance (*istighātha*) but impermissible to seek the assistance of another prophet or a saint.

Had the hadith been specific to this particular Companion, the Prophet ﷺ would have clarified this, just as he clarified to Abū Burda that a goat that was only six months old was permissible for him to ritually slaughter (*uḍḥiya*), but it was not permissible for other than him, and the soundness of this hadith is agreed upon by Bukharī and Muslim (*muttafaq ʿalayhi*).

'The Hadith of the Blind Man' has been referenced and authenticated by a number of recognised hadith masters and critics, such as Ibn Ḥajar al-ʿAsqalānī, Ibn Ḥajar al-Haytamī, al-Nawawī and al-Suyūṭī, amongst others, and narrated by Ibn Abī Khaythama and al-Tirmidhī, al-Ṭabarānī,

61 Fasting without opening the fast at sunset and continuing the fast the next day. – Tr.

al-Bayhaqī, al-Nasā'ī, ibn Mājah, al-Bukhārī in *al-Tarīkh,* Ibn Khuzayma and others.

Some people have tried to criticise this hadith since it constitutes clear evidence for the permissibility of *istighātha.* The scholars, however, have produced comprehensive refutations of the weak proofs which they have used.[62]

THE THIRD PROOF

The Companions made *istighātha* after the passing of the Prophet ﷺ and none of the other Companions condemned them for doing so. Ibn Ḥajar says in *Fatḥ al-Bārī,*[63]

> Ibn Abī Shayba narrates with a sound chain of transmission, from the narration of Abū Ṣāliḥ al-Sammān, on the authority of Mālik al-Dār, the treasurer of 'Umar ؓ, who said, 'People were afflicted by drought during the time of 'Umar b. al-Khaṭṭāb ؓ so a man came to the grave of the Prophet ﷺ and said, 'O Messenger of Allah! Seek rain for your nation or else they will perish.' So the Messenger of Allah ﷺ came to him in his dream and said, 'Go to 'Umar, give him greetings of peace and inform him that they will be granted rain and say to him, 'Do not be negligent' So the man went to 'Umar and informed him [of what had happened] and 'Umar ؓ cried and said, 'I will do everything in my power'

62 See *al-Radd al-Muḥkam al-Matīn,* p. 151
63 *Fatḥ al-Bārī,* p. 495, vol. II

The man was Bilāl b. al-Ḥārith al-Muzanī as Sayf narrates in *al-Futūḥ*. Look how this great Companion came to the grave of the Messenger ﷺ and he used to recite the same verses which people use today to declare Muslims as idolaters, yet he did not view his action as *shirk*.

Some people also criticise the hadith based on weak evidence.[64] Some say that the man who came to the grave of the Messenger ﷺ was not the great Companion Bilāl al-Muzanī but someone else who was unknown because Sayf's narration that says it was Bilāl al-Muzanī is subject to question.

The response to this is that even if the man was not Bilāl al-Muzanī, Sayyiduna 'Umar approved of him going to the Prophet's grave and calling upon him and he did not forbid him from doing so. If doing so had been *shirk*, would Sayyiduna 'Umar have approved of it?

Others reject this hadith by doubting the uprightness (*'adāla*) of Mālik al-Dār. To make this assertion is to question the judgement of Sayyiduna 'Umar and Sayyiduna 'Uthmān, both of whom put him in charge of the treasury.[65] It is inconceivable that someone who was not upright would be given this responsibility. It is sufficient that some of the

---

64 Critics of this hadith include Nāṣir al-Dīn al-Albānī who deemed this weak. However, Shaykh Muhammad Sa'īd Mamdūḥ wrote a lengthy refutation of al-Albānī's criticisms in his book, *Raf' al-Manāra* – Tr.

65 His name is Mālik b. 'Iyād but he was named Mālik al-Dār after being put in charge of the treasury. Imam al-Bukhārī included him in his *Tarīkh,* and he narrates on the authority of both Sayyiduna Abū Bakr and Sayyiduna 'Umar – Tr.

great scholars of hadith[66] said that he was well-known to be trustworthy (*thiqa*). The hadith is *ṣaḥīḥ* as Ibn Ḥajar al-ʿAsqalānī and other masters of hadith have said, so it is valid to use as proof for the permissibility of *istighātha.*

THE FOURTH PROOF

Imam al-Dārimī narrates with an authentic chain of transmission[67] that the People of Medina were afflicted by a severe drought, so they complained to Sayyida ʿĀ'isha ﷺ. She instructed them to go to the grave of the Prophet ﷺ and make an aperture in the ceiling such that the grave was open to the sky. They did this and it rained so heavily that the pasture flourished and the camels fattened until they were bursting (*fatq*) with fat, and the year became known as the Year of *Fatq*.

Reflect on this act which the Companions performed under the instruction of the wife of the Prophet ﷺ, and what it means. Sayyida ʿĀ'isha did not say to the Companions, 'Pray to Allah yourselves,' but rather she directed them to expose the noble grave to the heavens. Had there been even a trace of *shirk* in this, then Sayyida ʿĀ'isha would not have instructed them to do this, the Companions would not have

66 Amongst them Ibn Sa'd in his *Tabaqat*, and others

67 The hadith is *ṣaḥīḥ* according to Sayyid Ḥasan al-Saqqāf as the narrators are the same as Muslim's narrators, with the exception of ʿAmr b. Mālik al-Nakrī who is trustworthy (*thiqa*). Among the narrators is also Sa'īd b. Zayd, who some hold to be weak (*mutakallam fihi*), although Muslim narrates hadith on his authority. At the very least the hadith is *ḥasan* and is fit to be used as evidence.

accepted this and rain would not have fallen. However, they knew that this act, which is a type of *istighātha*, was acceptable and did not taint the purity of their faith in any way. In fact, such an act was a manifestation of their faith and thus did it without any objection.

THE FIFTH PROOF

In *Majmaʿ al-Zawā'id*, Imam al-Haythamī [68] relates the following hadith:

> On the authority of Khālid b. Saʿīd, on the authority of his father, on the authority of his grandfather who said, 'The tribe of Bakr b. Wā'il came to Mecca so the Prophet ﷺ said to Abū Bakr, 'Go to them and present Islam to them.' He went to them and they said, '[We will not consider your proposal] until our leader comes (who I think was al-Muthanna b. Khārija). So when he [their leader] arrived, he [Abū Bakr] asked them, 'Which tribe are you from?' They said, 'Banū Dhuhal b. Shaybān.' So Abū Bakr presented [Islam] to them and they said, 'We are currently at war with the Persians but when we have finished fighting them, we will consider what you said'.

68 *Majmaʿ al-Zawā'id wa Manbaʿl-Fawā'id*, by Nūr al-Dīn al-Haythamī (not to be confused with Ibn Ḥajar al-Haytamī). The narrators can all be found in the *Ṣaḥīḥ* collections except Khallād b. 'Īsā, who is trustworthy (*thiqa*)

> So when they came up against the Persians on the Day of Dhū Qār, their leader said [to his people], 'What is the name of the one who called you to Allah?' They said, 'Muhammad.' He said, 'He is your war cry.' They were given victory over their enemies and [when the Prophet ﷺ was informed of this] he said, 'Through me they were granted victory.'[69]

Look at how the Prophet ﷺ approved of the fact that they had made *istighātha* by him in his absence. He said, 'Through me they were granted victory.' Had *tawassul* or *istighātha* been *shirk*, then he would not have approved of them making *istighātha* by him. It is inconceivable that he would call them to leave idol worship and then know that they had made *istighātha* by him and then remain silent about it. This indicates that *istighātha* is permissible.

If someone were to reflect on these proofs and to scrutinise them they would come to the conclusion that even one of them is sufficient to prove the permissibility of *istighātha*, let alone all of them, as well as others which I have not

---

69 See *al-Sunnah wa'l-Bid'ah* by Sayyid 'Abdullāh b. Maḥfūẓ al-Ḥaddād

mentioned here.[70] They can be found in books such as *Shawāhid al-Ḥaqq* by al-Nabahānī, and *Nafas al-Raḥmān* by al-Ghirbānī, and *Mafāhīm Yajibu an tuṣaḥḥaḥ* [71] by Sayyid Muhammd ʿAlawī al-Mālikī, and *al-Wasīla li'l-Wiqāya ʿan Muḍillāt al-Fitan* by Ḥabīb Muhammad b. Sālim b. Ḥafīẓ.[72]

---

70 Such as the hadith that Ibn Mājah and others narrate on the authority of Abū Saʿīd al-Khuḍrī that the Messenger of Allah ﷺ said that if someone says upon going out to the prayer — "O Allah, I ask you by the right of those who ask of You, and by the right of my walking, for I do not leave in a state of pride or arrogance, nor out of ostentation or for the sake of reputation. I leave out of fear of Your punishment, hoping for Your pleasure. I ask You to protect me from the Fire and to grant me entry to Paradise, and to forgive my sins, for truly none can forgive sins except You" — Allah will appoint seventy thousand angels to seek forgiveness for him and will turn His countenance towards him until he finishes his prayer.

The scholars say that the hadith is evidence for the permissibility of making *tawassul* by the pious whether they be alive or dead. This is because their 'right' or status does not end when they die. Imam Ibn Khuzayma regarded the hadith to be *ṣaḥīḥ* and Ḥafiẓ ibn Ḥajar and others regarded it to be *ḥasan*. Some have tried to weaken the hadith on the basis of flimsy evidence.

71 Translated as *Notions That Must be Corrected* by ʿAbdul-ʿAzīz Surāqah – Tr.

72 In addition to *Raf' al-Manāra* by Sh. Muhammad Sa'īd Mamdūḥ which has already been mentioned, other lengthy works have been written, such as *al-Ta'ammul fī Ḥaqīqat al-Tawassul* by Sh. ʿĪsā b. Mānīʿ and *al-Tawassul bi'l-Ṣāliḥīn,* by Sh. ʿAbdul Fattāḥ Qudaysh. –Tr.

3

Rational Proofs for the Position of Ahl al-Sunna wa'l-Jamāʿa

HERE WE PRESENT THESE RATIONAL proofs for the position of *Ahl al-Sunna wa'l-Jamāʿa* on this issue. In reality, the fact that both *istighātha* and *tawassul* have been conveyed to us by universal continuous transmission (*tawātur*)[73] is sufficient proof in itself.

---

73 *Tawātur* is a level of transmission which reaches the highest degree of authenticity, such that it engenders certainty. In this context enough people narrate the performance of *istighātha* and *tawassul* in each generation that its permissibility and authenticity are beyond doubt.

THE FIRST PROOF

There was no debate about the issue of *istighātha* before the time of Shaykh Ibn Taymiyya,[74] so how should we regard Muslims who made *istighātha* before that time? The early generations, including the first three generations whose virtue is well known, made *istighātha* and *tawassul* and no-one condemned them for doing so. Among them were the renewers who Allah sends at the beginning of every century.[75] The fact that they made *tawassul* has been transmitted in their books and poetry as has their approval of others doing it. It is inconceivable that they were all idolaters.

THE SECOND PROOF

Had *istighātha* detracted from one's *tawḥīd* in any way then the friends of Allah, the elect of the Muhammadan Community would not have done it. How could they have reached the highest ranks of proximity to Allah whilst being in a state of disobedience to Him, let alone being idolaters?

Just as Allah protected the Prophets and Messengers from acts of disobedience, He protects His friends from acts of disobedience. Allah says, referring to the Devil, '*You*

---

74 The great scholar, Taqī al-Dīn al-Subkī said in his book, *Shifā al-Siqām*, 'Prior to Ibn Taymiyya, no-one from the early generations regarded *tawassul* to be reprehensible nor did anyone from the later generations. He said something that no scholar before him had ever said.'

75 The Messenger of Allah ﷺ said: "Allah will send to this nation at the beginning of every century someone who will renew its religion." This is a *ṣaḥīḥ* hadith narrated by Abū Dāwūd

have no authority over My slaves.'[76] The friends of Allah do not disobey Him. They are not infallible (*ma'ṣūm*) but they are protected (*maḥfūẓ*). It is conceivable for a saint (*walī*) to sin, but not a prophet.

The friends of Allah are people who are upright and who follow the Prophet ﷺ. They do not merely perform miracles. Miracles are in fact the result of following the Prophet ﷺ.

The early generations were the best generations and it is inconceivable that they could have fallen into *shirk* when the Prophet ﷺ gave them glad tidings as is mentioned in the *ṣaḥīḥ* hadith, 'The best of my nation is my generation, then those who follow them and then those who follow them.'[77]

We find in their biographies how they understood this issue and how they practised *tawassul*. An example of this is narrated by Imam al-Dhahabī in *Siyar A'lām al-Nubalā* in his biography of Ma'rūf al-Karkhī ﷺ, '"The grave of Mar'ūf is a proven cure (*tiryāq*)." He means by this that supplications are answered there, since supplications are answered in blessed places and at blessed times.'

THE THIRD PROOF

There is no explicit evidence to support the prohibition of *istighātha*, and the verses which people use as evidence do not in any way show that *istighātha* is prohibited or that it constitutes *shirk*. Furthermore the hadiths which they use

---

76 Qur'ān 15:42

77 Narrated by al-Bukhārī in the Chapter of the Virtues of the Companions

as evidence are weak and there is no authentic text (*naṣṣ*) which prohibits it.

Usury (*ribā*) is forbidden by consensus and the evidence for its prohibition is authentic and explicit and likewise fornication, drinking alcohol and severing the ties of kinship. Is it conceivable that *istighātha,* which its opponents claim constitutes idolatry, be a matter of scholarly debate, or that the evidence for its prohibition be unclear and inauthentic? Had the issue of *istighātha* been so serious, why were we left without clear evidence? Surely the warning against it would have been clear and unequivocal.

Conclusion

We have now presented the relied upon position of *Ahl al-Sunna wa'l-Jamāʿa* regarding the permissibility of *tawassul* and *istighātha*. It should be clear that making *tawassul* and *istighātha* does not detract from the purity of a person's belief in Allah's oneness. The performance of both *tawassul* and *istighātha* has been transmitted to us in a way which reaches *tawātur*,[78] from the pious and the prolific scholars of this nation – the jurists, the scholars of hadith, the Qur'ānic commentators and the scholars of legal theory and others.[79] Had *tawassul* and *istighātha* been prohibited, or had they constituted *shirk*, their performance would not have been transmitted to us from the standard-bearers of the Sacred Law. If the creed of such scholars was incorrect

78 See footnote 73
79 See *Shawāhid al-ḥaqq* by Imam Yūsuf al-Nabahānī

then the authenticity of the whole Sacred Law would be called into question.

We must hold a good opinion of Muslims in general and of the pious in particular. Such people are the standard-bearers of the pristine Sacred Law. They truly embody the Law and abide by its etiquettes. Through them, we know our great religion. They embody its realities and hold firm to its etiquettes. Anyone who reads their biographies[80] will appreciate their greatness, their scrupulousness, their detachment from the world, their knowledge and their miracles. They will then appreciate the greatness of the religion which such luminaries embodied, may Allah be pleased with them.

May Allah's mercy reach us, such that we witness great individuals who are beloved to Him and who are the inheritors of the Master of the progeny of ʿAdnān ﷺ. We ask that we witness them not with our physical eyes, since they are present amongst us, but that we witness them with our hearts after the veils have been lifted, veils which prevent us beholding them in reality, as Shaykh Abū Madyan ؓ, may we benefit from him said:

When shall I see them, and how may I see them
Or my ear hear news of them?

Who am I and how can someone like me share with them
In drinking from springs in which I find no impurity?

I love them, seek to please them and prefer them
Over my own self, specifically a group amongst them.

---

80 Such as *Ṭabaqāt al-Shāfiʿiyya al-Kubrā* by Ibn al-Subkī

They are a folk noble in character, wherever they sit
That place remains fragrant from their traces

Tasawwuf bestows (upon the seeker) a choice portion of their noble attributes
The intimacy which they display is a joy for me to behold

They are the ones for whom I reserve my affection, my loved ones
Who proudly bear the honour with which they have been invested.

(I ask) that I am constantly united with them for Allah's sake
And that our transgressions (against Him) be forgiven and pardoned

Then may blessings be bestowed upon the Chosen One, Our Master
Muhammad, the best of those who fulfil their vows. [81]

O Allah, we seek refuge in You from associating anything with You knowingly, and we seek Your forgiveness for that which we do unknowingly but of which You have knowledge, O Allah, O Generous (*Karīm*), O Merciful (*Raḥīm*), O Loving (*Wadūd*), O Living (*Ḥayy*), O Self-Subsisting (*Qayyūm*). We seek refuge in Allah from any thought that occurred to us, and from any desire that does

81 Taken from the ode, *The Sweetness of Life* by Shaykh Shuʿayb Abū Madyan and translated by Amin Buxton.

not please Allah whilst writing this work, or before it, or after it.

We ask Him for forgiveness, and that He replaces our bad deeds with good deeds O Allah! *'Our Lord! We believe, so forgive us our sins and protect us from the torment of the Fire!'*[82] *Our Lord, grant us good in this life and good in the hereafter and protect us from the torment of the Fire.'*[83]

---

82 Qur'ān 3:16

83 Qur'ān 2:201. Sayyidī al-Ḥabīb 'Alī b. 'Abdul-Raḥmān al-Jifrī once attended a gathering with Sayyidī al-Imam al-Ḥabīb 'Abdul-Qādir b. Aḥmad al-Saqqāf and al-Ḥabīb Aḥmad Mashhūr al-Ḥaddād and the latter said that he had not heard a Qur'ānic commentary of this verse that had satisfied him, so al-Ḥabīb 'Abdul-Qādir said *Our Lord, grant us good in this life,* means everything good that brings pleasure to the bodies, hearts, souls and inner secrets (*asrār*) and *good in the Hereafter,* means everything good that brings pleasure to the bodies or the hearts or the souls or the inner secrets. So al-Ḥabīb Aḥmad Mashhūr al-Ḥaddād said that he had never heard a better commentary than that.

I heard a commentary with a similar meaning from Sayyidī al-Imam 'Umar b. Muhammad b. Sālim b. Ḥafīẓ during a visit to the knower of Allah, al-Imam Ibrāhīm b. 'Umar b. 'Aqīl b. Yaḥyā in Ta'izz in the year 1411 AH. He narrated that al-Ḥabīb 'Abd al-Bārī b. Shaykh al-'Aydarūs said that *good in this life* is a pious wife and this is the portion of the body; the portion of the soul is time spent with one's brethren who one loves for the sake of Allah is and the portion of the inner secret (*sirr*) is knowledge of Allah. As for *good in the Hereafter,* the portion of the body is the maidens, palaces and the other pleasures of Paradise; the portion of the soul is gatherings in Paradise, as in the verse '*We will remove from their hearts all hatred; they will be as brothers facing one another on couches'* (Qur'ān 15:47) and the portion of the inner secret is the ecstasy of beholding Allah's noble countenance.

O Allah, we ask You for the good which Your slave and Prophet, Muhammad ﷺ and Your righteous slaves ask of You, and we seek refuge in You from the evil which Your slave and Prophet, Muhammad ﷺ and Your righteous slaves seek refuge from.[84]

We pray for those whose hearts have imbibed incorrect beliefs. May Allah save them from misguidance and allow us and them to recognise the sanctity of every believer. Allow us and them to die upon *Lā ilāha ill'Allāh Muḥammad Rasūlullāh.*

Let us conclude this treatise with this immense supplication. May Allah accept it despite of what is within us.

O Allah, make us people of *taqwā*, and let us be with the people of *taqwā*, and seal our lives with all goodness and certainty. Make us people who are rightly guided who guide others, O Most Generous.

These innovations which Muslims have fallen into are a tribulation and only You can remove it. O Allah, this tribulation has manifested itself in the guise of the Book and the Sunna but it has nothing to do with the Book and the Sunna. We ask that You guard Your Book and the Sunna of the Master of those beloved to You. We ask You by Your love for Your Book and by Your love for the Most Beloved of those Beloved that You accept this prayer and relieve us

---

84 This is a great supplication which many scholars have praised and placed in their litanies, including Imam ʿAbdullāh b. Ḥusayn b. Ṭāhir in his *Majmūʿ* and Imam Muhammad b. ʿAbdullāh al-Haddār

of this tribulation such that it disappears completely, and that none of the enemies of Islam achieve any of their goals.

This is our prayer, and You are the One who hears our prayers! O Allah, open the doors of relief, and remove every type of constriction and affliction. Turn to us and to the whole nation that we may sincerely repent and that our hearts, bodies and souls may be purified. Every day people are killed unjustly due to the effects of this tribulation, so we turn to You to relieve this distress and to transform our state.

O Allah, save them, for Your slaves are unable to do so. There is no refuge except in You and no salvation except by You. Other nations have summoned one another to attack this nation just as people invite others to share food, as Your Prophet ﷺ foretold.

O Allah, repel the evil of the disbelievers and evildoers and make us the best of people, those who remain firm upon the path of the Chosen One ﷺ. Make us the most felicitous of people and allow us to receive all goodness and increase, O Most Merciful.

May Allah send peace and blessings upon our master Muhammad, and upon his pure Family and Companions, the preservers of the religion, and those that follow them with excellence to the extent of Allah's knowledge.

To Allah belongs every kind of praise equal to the number of His created things, to His satisfaction, to the weight of His throne and to the the amount of ink required to record His words.

Appendix

Insights into Tawassul & Istighātha

BY HABIB UMAR BIN HAFIZ

BEAUTIFYING OUR APPROACH TO ALLAH

MAKING TAWASSUL BY THE PROPHETS and the elect slaves of Allah is built upon the firm foundation of seeking refuge in Allah and reliance upon Him. Someone who relies upon other than Allah has no need of an intermediary to seek Allah. Rather he will go straight to that other person and ask him and rely upon him. The person who takes someone as an intermediary, however, only uses this intermediary to strengthen and beautify his approach to Allah and to attain a bigger portion of Allah's compassion.

The beautification is affirmed in the Book and the Sunnah: '*O you who believe, fear Allah and seek a means to approach Him.*' [85] Allah commands us to seek a means to approach Him. Interpret it as you wish. If you in interpret

85 Qur'ān, 5:35

it to mean relying upon other than Allah then this will invalidate your knowledge as well as your actions. Interpret it as you wish. If you interpret the intermediary as your actions, then you and your actions are part of Allah's creation. Perhaps you should understand it to mean 'rely upon Me while using intermediaries that I have placed between you and Me to draw near to Me.' Interpret it as you wish, the fact is Allah has called us in His Book to use these means in order to strengthen our reliance upon Him and in order to beautify our approach to Him.

The Companions understood this concept and they thus beautified their approach to Allah by going to the Chosen One ﷺ. Allah says to us: '*If only when they wronged themselves they came to you and sought Allah's forgiveness and the Messenger sought forgiveness for them they would have found Allah Oft-Returning, Most-Merciful.*' [86]

'*Your Lord said: "Call upon me and I will respond to you."*' [87] People understand this verse to mean 'do not use the prophets as intermediaries.' This understanding is at odds with the Qur'ān and the Sunnah and at odds with the practice of the Prophet, the Companions and the Followers. This understanding has no basis. Allah says: '*If only when they wronged themselves they came to you...*' This is the first step – that they flee to you and turn to you realising your greatness. Allah could have said *and you sought Allah's forgiveness* and He forgave you and that would have been

86 Qur'ān, 4:64

87 Qur'ān 40:60

sufficient. But no, He said *and the Messenger sought forgiveness for them.*

What is this? This is Allah's way and Allah's religion. This is the way of the great scholars of the past. Is someone going to come along at the end of times and teach us his understanding of Allah's oneness? We have already taken our understanding from its source. Its light has been transmitted through flesh and blood century after century. This way was established by Muhammad ﷺ and the generations that followed lived by these principles, one knower of Allah after another, one scholar after another. All of them were truthful people, all of them were people drawn near to Allah and all of them renounced worldly things. These are the purest chains of transmission that we know.

A man came to the Messenger of Allah ﷺ and said: "I have gone blind so pray for me." In our time, if someone has a problem with their eyes they go to an eye specialist, but this man came to the Prophet. In that time they had no ordinary means to solve this problem. This was something that Allah alone could solve. This man came to the Prophet, knowing that no person was able to help him. The Prophet said: "If you wish, you can be patient and Paradise will be yours and if you wish, I will pray to Allah for you."

He replied: "I want Paradise and I want you to pray for me."

He expressed his feelings in the presence of the Prophet. The Companions knew what it meant to be in his presence. Had these sentiments been at odds with the correct understanding of Allah's oneness, this man was in the presence of the one who conveyed to them the correct understanding and defended this understanding from falsehood. But the Prophet did not disapprove of any of these sentiments. He told him to get up, perform ablution and perform two units of prayer. Then he told him to call on not one, but two: 'O Allah, I ask You and I turn to You through Your Prophet Muhammad ﷺ, the Prophet of mercy. O Muhammad!' Who was teaching him this? The one who taught us the meaning of Allah's oneness. The one who taught us who is Allah is. The one who called us to Allah. The one who conveyed the message. I do not need a shaykh from the east or the west, from Tihāmah or from Najd to come and teach me. I need Muhammad to teach me.

He taught him to say: 'O Muhammad, through you I turn to Allah.' He taught him to call upon Muhammad while Muhammad was not physically present. So he called upon Allah and called upon Muhammad and turned to Allah through him. He did not believe that Muhammad was his Lord or his god, but he knew that Muhammad was the Beloved of his Lord. He knew that Muhammad's station was above anyone else's station. He said: 'O Muhammad, through you I turn to Allah concerning this need of mine that it may be fulfilled.' The narrator of the hadith, 'Uthmān bin Ḥunayf, said: "By Allah, we had not yet dispersed and we had not talked for long before the man entered and he could see." The operation was over. No lasers were used. He prayed as he had been instructed and his sight returned.

The Prophet said (as is conveyed in a sound narration): 'If you have a need, then do as you have done.'

The Companions learnt this from the Prophet. A man came to 'Uthmān bin Ḥunayf during the caliphate of 'Uthmān bin 'Affān. He said: "I come to 'Uthmān bin 'Affān time and again with my need but I have not been able to speak to him. Ask him to speak to me." 'Uthmān bin Ḥunayf taught him to perform ablution and perform two units of prayer and to repeat the same prayer that the Prophet had taught the blind man. The man did this and returned the next day. There was no one at 'Uthmān bin Affān's door so he entered immediately and 'Uthmān received him, sat down with him and fulfilled his need. He told him to return whenever he had a need. The man left 'Uthmān's house and met 'Uthmān bin Ḥunayf in the street. He said to him: "May Allah reward you. After you spoke to 'Uthmān about me, he listened to me. Before that, he did not pay any attention to me."

'Uthmān bin Ḥunayf said: "I have not seen 'Uthmān since I spoke to you yesterday. I have not spoken to him. Did you do what I told you to do?"

"Yes," the man said.

"That is the reason your need was fulfilled." This was the result of making *tawassul* through the Prophet ﷺ. This was the understanding of the Companions.[88]

---

88 Extracts from a talk delivered by Ḥabīb Umar in Dar al-Mustafa, Tarim 5th Sha'bān 1434 AH

Regardless of what people say in this life regarding *tawassul*, every one of us will stand on the Day of Judgement. It is narrated in *Ṣaḥīḥ al-Bukhārī* that when people are in desperate need on that day they will go to Ādam but he will not help them. Then they will go to Nūḥ, then Ibrāhīm, then Mūsā and then ʿĪsā but none of them will help them. Not even the Prophets and Messengers dare to speak on that day. Each one of them says: 'My Lord's wrath has reached a level today which it has never reached before and it will never reach again. I am only concerned with my own salvation. Go to someone else!' Why do the Prophets say: 'Go to someone else?' Do they not understand the concept of Allah's oneness? Why do they not say: 'Ask your Lord. Allah does not need an intermediary between Him and His creation?' Adam says: 'Go to Nūḥ.' Why does he not say: 'Ask Allah?' Nūḥ says: 'Go to Ibrāhīm.' Not a single one of them says: 'Ask Allah directly.'

Here we come to realise the greatness of Allah's lordship. The likes of you and me and all our good actions are worth nothing. The only intermediary is the one who Allah loves and there is no one more beloved to Allah than Muhammad ﷺ. Allah wishes for us to know the station of His Beloved. This is why each prophet will pass people on to the next prophet, until the greatness of the Master of all the Prophets is made manifest. When they finally come to him he does not say: 'I am just a man like you. Do not seek help from a created being. Seek the help of the Creator!'

Rather he says: 'I am the one for this!' Perhaps you will hear this with your heart and your soul. This is so that you know how Allah causes His bounty to reach His slaves through those that He has drawn near and so that you know the station of Muhammad in Allah's sight.

Allah will say to them: 'Raise your head. Speak and you will be heard. Ask and you will be given. Intercede and your intercession will be accepted.' Only when the door of intercession is opened by Muhammad will the Prophets, the pious and the martyrs be able to intercede. Before that no prophet or martyr is able to speak: '*On that day, when the Spirit and the angels stand up in ranks, they will not speak; except he who is permitted by the Most Compassionate, and he will say what is right.*' [89] To whom will permission be given? It is only the Prophet ﷺ. He is the only one who will say: "I am the one for this!" May Allah give us an attachment to him which cannot be severed and allow us to live our lives loving him and following him.[90]

89 Qur'ān, 78:38

90 Extracts from a talk delivered by Ḥabīb Umar in Dār al-Muṣṭafā, Tarim 8h Rajab 1437 AH

NOTES